Kafui Koffi AKOLLY

From Health to Code: the Epic of an Innovator in eHealth

AF122888

Kafui Koffi AKOLLY

From Health to Code: the Epic of an Innovator in eHealth

ScienciaScripts

Imprint

Any brand names and product names mentioned in this book are subject to trademark, brand or patent protection and are trademarks or registered trademarks of their respective holders. The use of brand names, product names, common names, trade names, product descriptions etc. even without a particular marking in this work is in no way to be construed to mean that such names may be regarded as unrestricted in respect of trademark and brand protection legislation and could thus be used by anyone.

Cover image: www.ingimage.com

This book is a translation from the original published under ISBN 978-620-6-70540-6.

Publisher:
Sciencia Scripts
is a trademark of
Dodo Books Indian Ocean Ltd. and OmniScriptum S.R.L publishing group

120 High Road, East Finchley, London, N2 9ED, United Kingdom
Str. Armeneasca 28/1, office 1, Chisinau MD-2012, Republic of Moldova, Europe
Printed at: see last page
ISBN: 978-620-7-23880-4

Copyright © Kafui Koffi AKOLLY
Copyright © 2024 Dodo Books Indian Ocean Ltd. and OmniScriptum S.R.L publishing group

From Health to Code: The Epic of an Innovator in the eHealt_h_

Kafui K. AKOLLY
*Write**r***

From the same author :

Odyssey of a Soul Forged by Destiny, Autobiography, 2024

Table of contents

PREFACE 5
INTRODUCTION 6
PART 1: THE AWAKENING OF PASSION 7
    Chapter 1: The first echoes of a passion for printing in adolescence 7
    Chapter 2: Transition to IT as an alternative to printing 8
    Chapter 3: The challenges and opportunities of juggling healthcare and IT 9
PART 2: THE ESANTE TURNING POINT 11
    Chapter 1: Merging Two Worlds: Health and Digital 11
    Chapter 2: Ideation and planning : 13
    Chapter 3: Specifications 15
    Chapter 4: Choosing the development team 17
    Chapter 5: My personal experience in choosing developers 20
PART 3: PUTTING A DIGITAL PROJECT ON AN INSTITUTIONAL FOOTING.. 24
    Chapter 1: The legal basis of a digital project 24
    Chapter 2: My experience of institutional inking 26
PART 4: DEPLOYMENT 28
    Chapter 1: Choosing the application's technical features 28
    Chapter 2: Application testing 30
    Chapter 3: Official launch 31
    Chapter 4: Continuous updating 33
    Chapter 5: Presenting my eCentre Convivial digital project 34
PART 5: OUTLOOK 37
    Chapter 1: Future prospects for a digital application 37
    Chapter 2: Perspectives on the eCentre Convivial platform 37
PART 6: MOBILIZING RESOURCES 40
    Chapter 1: The importance of resource mobilization 40
    Chapter 2: Financial resources 41
    Chapter 3: Strategies for mobilizing financial resources 42
    Chapter 4: My success in mobilizing resources 43
    Chapter 5: Equity financing 44

Chapter 6: Subsidies from United Nations system agencies 44

Chapter 7: NFM2 & 3 grant (Global Fund) 45

Chapter 8: Competitions/Challenges 46

PART 7: ANALYSIS OF MY EXPERIENCE IN THE FIELD OF HEALTH IN AFRICA 50

Chapter 1: In-depth analysis of the eHealth context in Africa 50

Chapter 2: Specificities in the development of my project 52

Chapter 3: Obstacles encountered in developing my project 53

Chapter 4: Presenting the results of your work or research: an approach to visibility and networking 54

Chapter 5: Learning from success 64

Chapter 6: My role in the continued growth of this sector 65

CONCLUSION 66

Chapter 1: Taking stock 66

Chapter 2: Reflections 66

Chapter 3: Final messages and encouragement 68

Chapter 4: Epilogue 69

Chapter 5: Final thoughts on personal and professional development 70

POSTFACE 71

BIBLIOGRAPHY 72

From Health to Code: The Epic of an Innovator in eHealth

PREFACE

Through the pages of this captivating book, the reader is invited to plunge into the dynamic world of digital innovation, guided by the passionate author that I am, KAFUI KAFUI AKOLLY. Much more than a simple narrative of successes and challenges, this work is a vibrant testimony to the personal and professional evolution that comes from boldly exploring the digital world.

From the very first chapter, I take you on a journey from the genesis of an innovative idea to the concrete realization of a revolutionary application in the field of sexual and reproductive health. This story, rich in lessons learned, takes you behind the scenes of an entrepreneurial adventure where perseverance, adaptability and collaboration prove to be the pillars of success.

I'd like to share with you the lessons I've learned along the way, from mobilizing resources and working with developers, to the security of digital projects and the importance of maintaining rigorous ethics. Each challenge I overcome becomes an added stone in the construction of in-depth knowledge and a nuanced understanding of the field.

This book is not just a technical exploration; it also highlights the essential role of innovation in social, educational and economic transformation, particularly on the African continent. I share his concluding thoughts, inviting readers to pursue their vision, invest in their knowledge, celebrate their successes and protect their digital assets.

Whether you're a digital professional, a budding entrepreneur or simply passionate about innovation, this book offers valuable insight behind the scenes of digital creation and the keys to overcoming the challenges inherent in this constantly evolving field.

Kafui Kafui AKOLLY
Writer

INTRODUCTION

Dear readers, it's with great enthusiasm that I share with you my journey into the world of digital innovation. From the initial idea to the creation of a healthcare application, this journey has been punctuated by challenges, discoveries and successes. Over the years, I've learned the importance of collaboration, perseverance and security in the development of digital projects. In this narrative, I wish to share lessons learned from my experience and offer messages of encouragement to all those who aspire to create, innovate and positively impact the digital world. Join me for an enriching reflection on entrepreneurship, fruitful collaboration and the keys to success in digital innovation.

PART 1: THE AWAKENING OF PASSION

Chapter 1: The first echoes of a passion for printing in adolescence

Inside the 4ème classroom, my presence was motivated not only by the desire to assimilate the lessons being taught, but also by the role I had taken on as a service provider within my student community. In my school bag, I carried a variety of documents from different disciplines, meticulously bound, ready to be shared with my peers. I owed this habit in large part to my father, a printer by profession, who gave me the opportunity to put his skills to good use for my fellow students.

Thanks to this family connection to the world of printing, my fellow students were able to entrust me with their books and brochures, in need of meticulous binding, for a fee. But my services were not limited to simple binding. During this crucial period of adolescence, I also offered the reproduction of A5 calendars, printed on bristol paper, in black and white. This initiative proved particularly beneficial to many of my fellow girls, facilitating the discreet and practical management of their menstrual cycle. My school bag was not only the bearer of academic knowledge, but also the vehicle for practical services and unexpected community support.

My attraction to printing was deeply rooted, influenced by my father's talents and successes in the field. However, when we discussed my future plans, he dissuaded me from pursuing this passion, citing the unprofitability of the sector. This advice was colored by his own experience, marked by the bankruptcy of his first major printing company. Although I wasn't entirely convinced, I felt a filial obligation to follow his advice and abandon this path, for fear of repeating the difficulties he had encountered.

The bankruptcy of his company, which had occurred in the meantime, had undoubtedly influenced his perspective on the financial viability of the printing business. This personal experience had led him to discourage me, no doubt motivated by the fear that I might suffer the same fate. As his son, despite sharing a common passion, I eventually gave in to his recommendations, setting aside my aspirations to embrace a more conventional path, despite my lingering doubts.

So my dream of exploring printing as a career took a back seat, under the shadow of paternal concerns and the difficult economic realities he'd been through.

Chapter 2: Transition to IT as an alternative to printing

The awakening of my passion for computers goes back to the year 2000, marked by a self-initiated use of the Internet, particularly in Cybercafés. At the time, these establishments were ubiquitous in almost every neighborhood, offering a fascinating window onto the digital world. Memories of my early days are still linked to times when, while attending high school at my mother's, I would conscientiously sacrifice the money intended for my daily sustenance in order to subscribe to cybercafé services. Sometimes I was even forced to ask my mother for help when my resources ran out, as everything was invested in this quest for knowledge via the Internet. These early experiences in cybercafés not only forged my computer skills, but also inevitably led to financial compromises, symbolizing the determination of a young enthusiast ready to invest his modest budget in the quest for digital knowledge.

In my tireless quest to learn more about the world of the Internet, every free moment was devoted to exploring and browsing various websites, and exchanging e-mails with pen pals. The more time passed, the more fascinating opportunities and initiatives I unearthed. This daily process of discovery continually enriched my knowledge and skills in the field exponentially. Every day became a new page in my learning book, consolidating my growing expertise in this dynamic environment.

It was at this precise moment that I made my transition from printing to computers. Not only had I retained the skill of binding documents, but I had also developed an active expertise in word processing and graphic design, producing items such as greeting cards, business cards and invoices. So, at the age of 18, in class 1ère G2, I set up my very first company. As I went along, I applied the knowledge I'd acquired in accounting, general economics and organizational economics to this fledgling business, well aware of its fragility.

Chapter 3: The challenges and opportunities of juggling healthcare and IT

After my orientation towards associative life in 2004, my basic computer skills, acquired over time, proved invaluable. Thanks to specific training focused on sexual health and reproduction, the theme chosen for our associative action, I acquired the ability to enter texts and format professional documents independently. My involvement in the field of sexual and reproductive health was aimed at facilitating access to information and healthcare services for adolescents and young people. Targeting this particular population, with its dynamism and need for innovation, stimulated the search for innovative solutions and the bringing together of services to respond effectively to their specific needs.

Following the rise of social networking, I naturally turned my attention to this trend, seeking to transpose the initiatives I was already carrying out in the field. This transition led me to take charge of the animation of these networks by regularly publishing articles, boosted mainly on platforms such as Facebook and Google Ads. The sustained funding of this initiative by my partners, including the United Nations Population Fund (UNFPA), produced considerable results. This experience highlighted the speed with which social networks can reach the intended target, making a significant contribution to achieving the objectives set.

The fusion between my actions in the field and digital presence has been particularly fruitful. By investing in targeted campaigns, notably on Facebook and Google Ads, I was able to considerably amplify the reach of my initiatives. This synergy between the physical and virtual worlds demonstrated the power of social networks as a vector of influence and mobilization, while providing an effective platform for communicating, raising awareness and achieving the desired results.

At the heart of my approach was a major obstacle: data management and analysis. Although our active presence on social networks enabled us to reach a wide audience, the major constraint was the lack of access to the majority of target data, due to the non-proprietary nature of these platforms. This limitation had a significant impact on the sustainability of my approach, complicating data management and restricting my ability to make informed decisions. Thus emerged the pressing need for a private digital initiative, capable of overcoming the inherent limitations of social networks, by offering tighter data control, enhanced sustainability, and a solid foundation for future decision-making.

This challenge prompted me to look beyond the social networking channel. Despite their considerable reach, dependence on these external platforms was becoming a handicap to our autonomy. So the idea of a private digital initiative took shape, with the vision of going beyond the limits imposed by social networks. This initiative was aimed at offering much more personalized services, ensuring more efficient data management, guaranteeing sustainability in actions and providing a solid basis for future strategic decisions. Hence a digital eHealth application.

PART 2: THE ESANTE TURNING POINT

Chapter 1: Merging Two Worlds: Health and Digital

Now that you have a glimpse of how I got my start in the digital world, particularly in the field of eHealth, I'm going to share through my stories my journey as an eHealth promoter and my analysis of the situation. My aim is to set out an enlightened path for those who are already in this field or who aspire to move into it. My immersion in the digital world was the result of a natural evolution, from my early interest in computing to my involvement in sexual and reproductive health initiatives. Through these experiences, I developed a variety of skills, navigating between IT, social networks and, finally, eHealth. These transitions have offered me unique perspectives on how technology can be integrated to positively influence health and well-being.

In the course of my career, I have been confronted with significant challenges, including data management in the field of digital health. These challenges have been catalysts for the creation of private digital-focused initiatives aimed at overcoming the limitations of social networks. My story will detail these steps, while offering insights and advice for those wishing to navigate the complex but promising world of eHealth. As you can see, there are a few peculiarities to my story. On the one hand, I don't have a degree in medicine, my training being limited mainly to preventive medicine, with active participation alongside healthcare providers in our field activities focusing on advanced strategies. On the other hand, I didn't study software engineering, so I can't claim the privilege of developing a digital application myself.

My involvement in preventive medicine activities has been a rich learning ground, enabling me to understand the issues and challenges of the health sector, in particular sexual and reproductive health. At the same time, although I didn't formally study software engineering, my path in digital enabled me to collaborate with experts in application development, strengthening my understanding of technical aspects without possessing in-depth programming expertise. I share this testimonial to underline the crucial importance of understanding the field you're getting involved in, especially when it comes to digital application development, especially when it's associated with a theme as complex and delicate as healthcare.

When developing a healthcare-focused digital application, a thorough understanding of medical needs, care protocols and operational challenges is fundamental. Consequently, my testimony underlines the importance of collaborating with experts in each relevant field. By combining my healthcare knowledge with technical skills, I was able to contribute to the development of a digital application that effectively meets the needs of the healthcare sector. This reinforces the idea that success in the digital field, especially in sensitive sectors such as healthcare, depends on close collaboration between varied and complementary profiles.

Digital innovation requires two major components to ensure the success of a project: a thorough knowledge of code and an in-depth understanding of the specific theme, whether it be health, education, finance, housing, transport, culture, society, and many others. Mastering code is essential, as it enables ideas to be transformed into digital reality. Understanding programming languages, software architectures and the principles of web or application development is fundamental to turning innovative concepts into reality. It's the technical foundation that brings digital solutions to life and enables them to be adapted to the specific needs of the chosen field.

By combining these two components, the digital innovator can create solutions that are not only technically robust, but also precisely meet the real needs of the society in which they are deployed. It is this synergy between technical mastery and contextual understanding that defines the success of digital innovation projects. This technical competence enables the digital innovator to materialize his or her ideas, create applications, websites or other digital solutions, thus laying a solid foundation for the realization of innovative concepts.

Along the way, I've had the opportunity to meet doctors and healthcare professionals involved in eHealth projects, but who were held back in their progress by their lack of knowledge of the coding field. At the same time,

I've come across developers with great ambitions in the healthcare sector, but who have failed to win the support of partners or users due to their lack of knowledge of the healthcare sector and, more broadly, of the various laws governing this field. These experiences highlight the crucial importance of close collaboration between healthcare professionals and development experts. Physicians, with their clinical expertise, bring an in-depth understanding of patient needs, medical protocols, and the challenges specific to the healthcare sector. Developers, for their part, translate this knowledge into concrete digital solutions, using their coding expertise.

In this book, which also acts as a guide, I share in detail my personal journey and reveal how I succeeded, even without the background of the two aforementioned actors. What I would describe as a transition from amateur to professional. I explore the challenges I encountered as I immersed myself in the world of eHealth, highlighting initial gaps in my knowledge, including a lack of formal medical skills and in-depth coding training. Despite these obstacles, I share how my passion, determination and ongoing commitment to learning shaped my evolution into an accomplished professional in the field.

This authentic story aims to inspire other aspiring digital innovators, demonstrating that with the right attitude, perseverance and a consistent learning approach, even those without traditional backgrounds can thrive and succeed in such demanding sectors as eHealth.

Chapter 2: Ideation and planning :

In 2017, when analyzing my initiatives with social networks, I began informal approaches to state partners and donors to present my idea of creating an eHealth app. The aim was to put our country on the map of innovation in this field. I initiated discussions with potential players who shared my vision and the importance of combining technological advances with the needs of the healthcare sector. My ambition was to help improve healthcare services by taking advantage of the opportunities offered by digital technology. These first steps marked the beginning of what was to become an exciting journey into the world of eHealth.

In this approach, the aim was to transpose the proposals of various existing policies and programs into digital form, without trying to invent something totally new. I therefore initiated discussions with organizations such as UNFPA, SP/CNLS and UNAIDS. These exchanges took the form of personal interviews and the transmission of a project sheet. The aim was to present how an eHealth application could be aligned with existing sexual and reproductive health objectives. The aim was to capitalize on existing efforts and add a digital dimension to reinforce the effectiveness of health interventions.

Alongside this initiative, I took it upon myself to initiate discussions with a variety of people, ranging from acquaintances to friends, colleagues and, above all, the beneficiaries of our actions. The aim was to gather their opinions and suggestions. This participatory approach aimed to incorporate the varied perspectives of those who would be directly impacted by an eHealth application. The feedback and ideas gathered enriched the project's vision, enabling a deeper understanding of the community's real needs and expectations. This was a crucial step in ensuring that the application would be truly adapted and beneficial to those it was intended to serve.

This is of crucial importance, particularly as the project needs to win the support of political players, partners and users. It provides an opportunity to anticipate possible resistance and determine how to consolidate the project by creating a solid block of partners. Exploring the opinions and suggestions of different stakeholders enables potential concerns to be identified and proactively addressed. This encourages consensus-building and the establishment of a support network from the earliest stages of the project. By understanding the varied perspectives and integrating the needs of all parties, the project can be positioned to win buy-in and establish fruitful partnerships.

Indeed, many innovators neglect this crucial step in their approach. In the eyes of partners and especially decision-makers, particularly at national level, an approach perceived as imposing faits accomplis can lead to a reluctance to provide support. Prior dialogue and consultation with stakeholders is essential to establish a basis for understanding and collaboration. Ignoring this step can give the impression that the project is being developed in isolation, without taking into account the perspectives and concerns of key stakeholders. By incorporating these voices from the outset, innovators can better position their initiative to gain strong, lasting support.

In my case, after unofficially approaching the various partners, I had to draw up the project document in which I explained what this digital project was and what it would contribute to for teenagers and young people. So far, it's not about the specifications of the application. It's gratifying to note that this approach has been welcomed and endorsed by the various partners involved. This not only strengthened the credibility of the project, but also provided essential reassurance at every stage of the application development process.

Partner approval and support confirms the validity of the vision and reinforces the legitimacy of the project. This foundation of credibility, gained through open and transparent collaboration, creates an environment conducive to the continued success of the application's development.

Chapter 3: Specifications

A specification is a document detailing the project's specifications, functionalities, technical requirements and constraints. It serves as a common reference between stakeholders (customers, developers, etc.) to ensure a clear understanding of expectations and guarantee consistency throughout the development process. Indeed, it is regrettable that many innovators and developers undertake the development of an application without a detailed specification. This can have a detrimental effect on the quality of the process.

A well-developed specification plays a crucial role in providing a clear vision and structured framework for the project. It defines expectations, specifications and constraints, providing a solid foundation for the entire development process. The absence of this document can lead to misunderstandings, differing interpretations and ineffective communication between stakeholders. These shortcomings can ultimately lead to delays, additional costs and, in some cases, compromise the final quality of the product. It is therefore strongly recommended that innovators and developers recognize the importance of well-developed specifications in ensuring the success and quality of their application projects.

It's only fair to emphasize the importance of specifications prior to the implementation of any digital project. The initial responsibility for drawing up this document generally lies with the innovator. In the absence of this competence on the part of the innovator, the task can be entrusted to the developer, provided the latter possesses in-depth knowledge of the project's subject matter. If this is not the case, it is advisable to call in an expert or to organize workshops involving both those involved in the specific project theme and developers. This collaboration ensures a clear understanding of expectations and requirements, contributing to the creation of solid specifications, aligned with the real needs of the project and guaranteeing successful implementation.

In my particular situation, I had originally confused the project document with the specifications. It was during discussions with the developers, who were raising points that were not in the project document, that I realized the importance of writing a separate specification. Fortunately, this task didn't turn out to be as difficult as expected, especially as I have a natural penchant for writing and a thorough understanding of the subject I wanted to explore through this application.

A specification for the development of a digital application should include:

- ***Introduction and Objectives*** : Presents the context of the project, the reasons for its creation, and the specific objectives to be achieved.

- ***General project description:*** Provides an overview of the product, identifies its target audience, and explains how it will meet user needs.

- ***Functional requirements:*** Lists the specific functionalities that the application must offer, e.g. graphic design, user registration, data management, etc.

- ***Non-functional requirements:** These* include constraints related to performance, security, compatibility with other systems, and other aspects not directly linked to functionality.

- ***User interface (UI/UX):*** Details the application's visual design, user interactions, and may include mock-ups to illustrate the concept.

- ***Technical requirements:*** Specifies programming languages, frameworks, databases and other technological elements to be used in development.

- ***Data management:*** Explains how data will be stored, processed and retrieved, including a description of the database structure.

- ***Security:*** Identifies the security measures needed to protect the application against potential vulnerabilities and guarantee data confidentiality.

- ***Testing and validation:*** Details test methods for each feature, acceptance criteria, and plans for final product validation.

- ***Deliveries and schedules:*** Divide the project into phases, set milestones for each phase, and define expected delivery dates.

- ***Budget and resources:*** Estimate the costs associated with development, allocate the necessary resources (human, material, etc.), and identify any budgetary constraints.

- ***Contractual terms:*** Includes the terms and conditions of the contract, the responsibilities of the parties, and any termination clauses.

Chapter 4: Choosing the development team

The crucial stage in developing a digital solution inevitably involves identifying a developer or a team of developers, depending on the specific needs of the project. This collaboration is essential to transform the innovator's vision into a functional, interactive reality. The choice of developer is particularly important, as he or she must not only master the technical aspects of coding, but also understand the underlying theme of the project. Indeed, the success of a digital application depends on the symbiosis between the creator's vision and the developer's skills, an alliance that shapes the development path and guarantees the quality of the final result.

Collaboration between the innovator and the developer often extends to a group of specialized stakeholders, each contributing to a specific aspect of the project. Ideally, the group includes a specialist in the subject matter, ensuring a thorough understanding of the needs of the field in question. A web designer creates a visually appealing interface, while a front-end developer makes the application accessible and interactive for the user. A back-end developer is responsible for data management and application logic on the server side. It should be noted that, in certain situations, a single developer may combine design, back-end and front-end skills, depending on the scale and specific requirements of the project. This diverse team guarantees a holistic approach to digital development.

The process of identifying the development team is of crucial importance in the innovator's journey. After careful selection, it's essential that the developer works closely with the team to ensure a shared, in-depth understanding of the project. This step promotes clarity of expectations, aligning everyone's objectives and ensuring a shared vision. Constant communication between the innovator and the development team helps prevent potential misunderstandings and maintain a consistent direction throughout the process.

Once the development team has been identified and selected, the next step is to sign the contractual documents that will govern the application's development. This stage is of paramount importance in clearly defining the terms, responsibilities and expectations of each party involved. The contractualization process must be rigorous, emphasizing clear objectives, deadlines and quality criteria. These contractual documents provide a solid framework, establishing common ground between the innovator and the development team, and laying the foundations for a fruitful collaboration. Rigor in this phase helps to minimize risk, ensure mutual understanding and secure the path to successful application development.

When developing a digital application, it's essential to clarify the legal aspects of intellectual property, particularly with regard to source code. In my experience, I've been confronted with situations where certain developers were unaware of the terms of the transfer of rights. That's why, right from the start of the contractualization process, I took care to include specific clauses on source code ownership. The aim of these clauses is to ensure that the rights to the codes revert to the project sponsor, in this case myself as the innovator, once the paid work has been completed. This approach prevented any misunderstandings and secured my rights to the final product, contributing to a more transparent and harmonious collaboration with the development team.

Contractualization in the development of digital applications requires precise documentation to avoid misunderstandings and ensure that the interests of all parties involved are protected. Here is a list of essential contractual documents when working with a developer:

1. ***Rights assignment contract***: This document clearly establishes the terms of intellectual property, specifying that the source codes developed belong to the project sponsor after remuneration of the developer.

2. ***Specifications***: This is a detailed document describing the project's specifications, functionalities and requirements. It provides a common reference to ensure consistency throughout the development process.

3. ***Service contract***: This contract specifies the obligations, deadlines and payment terms between the parties. It establishes the responsibilities of each party and ensures a clear understanding of expectations.

4. ***Confidentiality agreement (NDA)***: An NDA is often essential to protect sensitive information exchanged during development. It ensures the confidentiality of project details.

5. ***Work plan or chronogram***: A detailed schedule of the work to be carried out, milestones and deadlines enables you to monitor the project's progress and ensure that deadlines are met.

By taking care to incorporate these elements into contractual documents, clear working relationships can be established, minimizing risks and ensuring transparent collaboration with the various stakeholders. However, depending on the specific nature of the project and the stakeholders involved, other contractual documents may be necessary to ensure clear understanding and efficient execution.

Chapter 5: My personal experience in choosing developers

My experience in identifying developers was comparable to a baby's first hesitant steps, where each fall was followed by renewed determination to move forward. Initially, I asked a group of young software engineering students to join the project. Among them were a web designer and two developers. Unfortunately, this collaboration ended in failure, mainly due to a failure to keep to the schedule, a misinterpretation of the specifications, and an obvious lack of experience on the part of these young developers. These problems inevitably led to an abrupt termination of the contract. The consequences were significant: expenses were incurred, but no tangible results were achieved.

It's important to note that, at the outset, the development of this application was financed entirely from our own resources. Although some aspects of the theme received partial financial support from the United Nations Population Fund (UNFPA), the actual development expenses were covered entirely by internal resources. This approach denotes a significant initial commitment, where personal funds were invested in bringing the idea to fruition, underlining dedication and conviction to the project. The decision to finance the development of the application in-house was motivated both by the partner's financial constraints and by the desire to ensure autonomy while preserving the application's intellectual property. This approach was supported by the Global Fund.

My second attempt at recruiting developers turned to a qualified group of experienced professionals. Unfortunately, this collaboration also ended in failure, mainly due to a faulty interpretation of the specifications and problems with the deliverables. This resulted in a further series of expenses, in line with the terms of the established contract. These experiences reinforced my understanding of the challenges inherent in the application development process, highlighting the complexity of working with external teams. Faced with the reality of unsatisfactory work and the passage of time, I was forced to categorically cancel the contract with the group of developers, demanding repayment of the funds previously advanced. This involved several stages of recovery, but I finally obtained restitution of the funds. These twists and turns strengthened my perseverance and served as a valuable lesson in the rigorous selection of service providers and the meticulous management of contracts in the field of application development.

The search for the ideal service provider for the development of my initiative required up to five contractualization attempts. It was finally during the last attempt that I had the good fortune to meet a promising young talent by the name of Vokou Kokou Rodrigue. A software engineer, he stood out for his calm and attentive spirit, demonstrating an acute understanding of the application's stakes and a clear apprehension of the challenges that lay ahead for both him and me. This partnership marked a decisive turning point in the development of the application, symbolizing a timely encounter with a competent and committed collaborator.

Unlike a team of developers, this young talent set himself apart by acting as an individual, effectively taking on the role that would normally have fallen to an entire team. He didn't hesitate to openly communicate his limits and questions, thus establishing a relationship of transparency and collaboration. Working with Vokou Kokou Rodrigue was an eye-opener, making me realize that developing this application also required a basic understanding of development basics. I also understood that the developer himself could not design an algorithm without a prior mastery of the specific theme, in this case sexual and reproductive health. This realization not only clarified my role as initiator, but also underlined the crucial importance of the synergy between the thematic field and development skills in the creation of a successful digital application.

Let's illustrate this with the example of integrating the menstrual cycle tracking service into the application. This particular service requires in-depth mathematical expertise to avoid any tracking errors. What's more, writing a complete algorithm for this tracking requires a thorough understanding of the menstrual cycle. So anyone who lacks both knowledge of the menstrual cycle and math skills cannot successfully complete this crucial part of the project. On the strength of my in-depth understanding of the subject and my math skills, I took the initiative in formulating the hypotheses and writing the algorithm for tracking the menstrual cycle in the application. This process was the fruit of my collaboration with the developer, to whom I passed on the algorithm, which he then translated into his computer language. This approach was consistently applied to other services integrated into the application, demonstrating that synergy between technical and thematic skills is essential at every stage of development.

In order to avoid past mistakes and ensure more efficient budget management, I took the strategic decision to sign a results-oriented contract with the new developer. In concrete terms, the terms of this contract were clear: no payment would be made until the agreed work had been completed, delivered and validated. This approach was intended to create a dynamic of responsibility and commitment, encouraging the developer to deliver quality results, while enabling me to secure the funds invested. This choice of contractualization was essential to ensure the success of the project and minimize financial risks.

For almost a year, a close and fruitful collaboration took shape between the developer and myself. Together, we worked tirelessly to bring to fruition this beautiful innovation, a first in Togo's history. This intense period was marked by constant exchanges, meticulous adjustments and continuous alignment with the project's objectives. The fusion of our respective skills enabled us to overcome technical and conceptual challenges, resulting in the creation of an application that would have a significant impact in the field of digital health in Togo.

PART 3: THE INSTITUTIONAL FRAMEWORK FOR A DIGITAL PROJECT

Chapter 1: The legal basis of a digital project

Plunging into the adventure of a digital innovation project, whether in the field of eHealth or other digital themes, requires the project owner to have legally recognized institutional coverage. This crucial step is the foundation on which the project's credibility and viability rest.

There are two main options for securing institutional coverage for your project: setting up a civil society organization, such as an association, or creating a company (sole proprietorship, corporation, etc.). These days, setting up one of these two structures is relatively straightforward. Once the status has been defined, official registration of the entity with the relevant authorities is imperative. This gives the project a legal existence and enables it to benefit from the rights and duties associated with its status. For those who opt to set up a business, a question frequently raised concerns the management of taxes, especially when the company does not yet have the necessary financial capacity. Legal instruments exist to simplify this process. Generally speaking, all that's required is to declare the company's inactivity within the time limits laid down by the country's tax legislation. This step is designed to protect the company in the process of being set up, thus avoiding potential problems with the tax authorities.

For projects involving specific innovations or developments, intellectual property protection is essential. This may include filing patents, trademarks or other appropriate forms of protection. And depending on the nature of the project, it's crucial to comply with current sector-specific regulations. In the case of eHealth, for example, there may be specific standards to be met to guarantee the security and confidentiality of medical or personal data.

To sum up, setting up a solid, regulatory-compliant institutional structure is a prerequisite for any digital innovation project. It provides the project owner with the legal certainty and confidence needed to evolve in an often complex environment. A large number of digital promoters are looking for partners or are already promoting their solutions to the public, without fulfilling the crucial condition of having an institutional base. This gap represents a major risk factor and can discredit the project, particularly in the eyes of partners and authorities. These may include :

1. ***Legal risks***: The absence of a legally recognized entity exposes the project to significant legal risks. Potential litigation, unfulfilled obligations and conflicts with third parties could have adverse consequences for the project's long-term viability.

2. ***Partner confidence***: Potential partners, whether financial, technical or strategic, attach great importance to institutional credibility. A project backed by a formal structure is perceived as more reliable, which favors the establishment of solid partnerships.

3. ***Authorizations and accreditations***: Certain sectors, particularly those related to healthcare, require specific authorizations and may require accreditation. Without an adequate institutional base, obtaining these authorizations may be hampered, bringing the project to a halt.

4. ***Public legitimacy***: In the eyes of the general public, an institutionally anchored initiative gains in legitimacy. Users, whether individuals or organizations, are more inclined to trust and adopt solutions from established, recognized entities.

5. ***Regulatory Compliance***: Compliance with current regulations is essential, especially in sensitive areas such as healthcare. An institutional entity finds it easier to adapt and comply with legislative changes, which reinforces project compliance.

6. ***Attractiveness for investors***: To attract investors, it is essential to present a robust institutional framework. Investors are more inclined to support projects that have a sound legal framework, thereby minimizing the risks associated with the investment.

Indeed, institutional anchoring goes beyond simply naming the organization. It requires the establishment of a physical infrastructure, even if it's just a room or two, to enable the structure to function effectively. This physical presence helps to establish a solid basis of trust with the project's various stakeholders, be they potential partners, collaborators or the authorities. It reinforces the project's legitimacy and credibility, demonstrating the promoter's serious commitment to his digital initiative.

Chapter 2: My experience of institutional inking

In my particular situation, I was fortunate enough to already have a legally recognized association. Having deliberately left my position as ICT Assistant at the Country Office of the United Nations Industrial Development Organization (UNIDO) after eight years' experience, my office also served as the headquarters for my association. My decision was to devote myself fully and full-time to my digital project, demonstrating my total commitment to the eHealth initiative I was spearheading.

Faced with this situation, I found myself somewhat isolated, without a physical location to house the headquarters of my association and, by extension, my digital innovation. This, despite the agreement in principle already obtained from my partners. It therefore became imperative to actively look for premises, thus ensuring the continuity of the process and providing an operational base for myself and my collaborators.

Fortunately, providence has always seemed to watch over me, and at a critical moment, I discovered a call for applications for incubation of projects aimed at promoting the female gender. This precious call came from the Innov'up incubation center. Without hesitation, I submitted my application and was selected following interviews. It was the start of 2018, marking an exciting new chapter for my organization. During my incubation at Innov'up, my structure benefited from a cubicle equipped with a computer, three chairs, and all the logistical tools necessary for our work. This opportunity gave us a functional space in which to develop our project. At the same time, I had access to a team of business support experts at the center, including an accountant, a human resources manager, a project manager and a web designer. This provision of specialized human resources considerably strengthened my operational capacity and professionalism in leading this initiative.

With these favorable conditions, I was able to successfully complete the rest of my application development path, with particular emphasis on mobilizing the necessary resources. The presence of experts at Innov'up also helped me refine my strategic approach to financial management and project planning.

PART 4: DEPLOYMENT

Chapter 1: Choosing the application's technical features

In the process of developing a digital project, it is very important for the innovator to make strategic decisions on the following aspects:

- **Domain name**: Choose a relevant and memorable domain name, taking into account availability and relevance to your project.

- **Server**: Select the type of server that meets your needs, whether dedicated, shared or cloud-based.

- **Programming language**: Choose the right language for your project, depending on the type of functionality you want to implement.

- **Database**: Choose the database best suited to your application, depending on the complexity and volume of data to be managed.

- **Framework**: Use a framework compatible with your chosen language, which can speed up development by providing a pre-established structure.

- **Security**: Implement robust security measures, including data encryption, access management and protection against vulnerabilities.

- **Hosting**: Choose the right type of hosting for your project needs, whether shared, dedicated or cloud-based.

- **Version management**: Use a version management system such as Git to track code changes and facilitate collaboration.

- **Backup and recovery**: Implement regular backup strategies to protect your data from accidental loss.

- **Monetization (if applicable)**: If your project has a commercial aspect, determine the appropriate monetization methods, whether through advertising, subscriptions or other means.

- **Legal compliance**: Make sure you comply with all applicable laws and regulations, particularly in terms of data protection and confidentiality.

Differences may arise between the sponsor and the developer during this process. Some developers make the mistake of acquiring domain names or servers in their own name, or even of allocating space on their server to the client. This can cause problems if the client wishes to take over project management autonomously, thereby incurring unnecessary costs and risks. It's essential to establish clear conditions of ownership and access to technical resources right from the start of the project to avoid such disagreements. As a developer, not a host, it is imperative to guarantee the independence of each customer's project, and to assign rights in full in accordance with the terms of the contract. As a general rule, the right of assignment should revert to the customer, ensuring clarity and transparency over the project's intellectual property. This approach eliminates potential risks associated with the management of technical resources, and avoids any misunderstandings as to the ownership of the project developed.

Integrating a database into your digital project is of crucial importance, and is often a differentiating factor in a competitive context. The database is essential for efficiently storing, organizing and retrieving the information needed to make your application or solution work. Surprisingly, many innovators or developers overlook the fundamental aspect of data management by not incorporating a database into their solution. The ability to interact with beneficiaries and providers relies heavily on the availability and efficient management of data.

A well-designed database will not only store information in a structured way, it will also facilitate the implementation of interactive functionalities. This can include user profiles, activity histories, feedback, and other key elements required for a rich user experience.

It's crucial to make the right choices when it comes to technical features, as they will determine the smooth running and performance of your project. These choices depend closely on the nature and scope of your digital initiative. Every project has its own specific requirements in terms of technology, architecture and functionality.

To begin with, the very nature of your digital application or solution will influence the type of platform or framework you choose. For example, a healthcare-focused project might require specific functionality related to medical data management, while an educational platform might call for interactive learning features. Project size also comes into play, as a small-scale project may opt for lighter, more agile solutions, while a large-scale project is likely to require a more robust and scalable infrastructure. It's essential to strike a balance between required functionality, scalability and available resources.

Direct management of the server interface and domain name for my application was a strategic decision. As the developer, I occupied a central position by having exclusive control over the highest level of access. I had deliberately granted partial access to the developer, limited to the specific needs of his work on the project. This approach was designed to guarantee a monopoly and total control over the project, ensuring its security and sustainability. By maintaining tight control over the technical infrastructure, I was able to make rapid decisions, make changes in real time and react effectively to any problems.

Project security was a major concern, and the exclusive management of access levels was a preventive measure to avoid unauthorized access. This also helped to protect sensitive data, preserve confidentiality and guarantee operational continuity.

Chapter 2: Application testing

The initial phase of application testing is carried out first by the developer himself, then in collaboration with the project sponsor. This process is generally integrated throughout the development process, step by step. This approach makes it easier to anticipate programming errors and bugs, thus guaranteeing the stability of the entire project once completed. The developer carries out rigorous testing as he completes each stage of development, identifying and resolving problems as he goes along.

The next step is to extend these tests by involving the project sponsor. This collaboration between the developer and the sponsor aims to validate specific functionalities, ensure that the requirements of the specifications are met, and gather feedback from the future user. In short, this progressive approach to testing, combining the developer's expertise and the client's perspectives, ensures the reliability of the project and minimizes the risk of major corrections once development is complete. Subsequently, testing can be extended to a restricted group, extended to include family members, acquaintances, not forgetting the partners directly involved in the project. The main aim of this application testing phase is to identify any inconsistencies and gather user feedback, with a view to making significant improvements.

Once these preliminary stages have been completed, a crucial step in the full development of the project is the launch of a Beta test. This test can be aimed at a wider audience, with particular emphasis on the application's target audience. It offers the opportunity to gather wider feedback, identify specific problems related to actual use of the application, and ensure that the overall system meets end-users' expectations. The Beta testing period therefore represents a decisive phase for fine-tuning the application before its full roll-out, incorporating user feedback to guarantee an optimal experience for the official launch.

Following the success of these various test phases, the long-awaited moment has come to bring this innovation to market. This marks the official launch of the application. This marks a major turning point in the development process, symbolizing the application's transition from a project in progress to a product available to the general public.

Chapter 3: Official launch

The official launch is an opportunity to present the application to the target audience, partners, the media and anyone interested in this new digital solution. It is usually accompanied by a communications campaign to publicize the application, generate excitement and attract potential users. This is a crucial moment when the promoter can measure the impact of his innovation on the market and begin to gather initial feedback from users. Before proceeding with any further steps, it is imperative to ensure that the innovation meets the regulatory requirements in force in the territory of action. The support of partners and authorities is also crucial to the project's success. This process of regulatory compliance and institutional approval is often overlooked, but it is a fundamental step in avoiding potential obstacles and guaranteeing project sustainability. Many promising digital innovations have failed for lack of adherence to existing standards and regulations, highlighting the importance of this preliminary precaution.

The official launch of my eCentre Convivial project was a crucial moment, marked by a series of strategic steps and lobbying. Thanks to a clear endorsement from UNFPA, I was able to benefit from the support of the entire UN system in Togo, including UNDP and UNAIDS, as well as the Global Fund to Fight AIDS, Tuberculosis and Malaria. This close collaboration with UN agencies has strengthened my commitment to the State, in particular with the Ministry of Youth and the Ministries of Education, contributing to the adhesion of the Ministry of Health and the Ministry of Digital Economy.

This strategic approach created synergy between the public sector, international organizations and my initiative, establishing a solid foundation for the official launch of the project. Collaboration with health authorities and related ministries was crucial to ensure the smooth integration of innovation into the national health and Digital landscape.

The presence of various government institutions demonstrates the institutional support given to the application, reinforcing its legitimacy and credibility. This milestone marks a significant turning point in the realization of the initiative, paving the way for its effective deployment in the health and eHealth sectors in Togo.

Chapter 4: Continuous updating

Introducing the need for an update in the context of promoting an eHealth application is necessary to understand the stakes and benefits associated with this process. In the field of digital health, rapid technological advances and ever-changing regulatory requirements mean that applications must be constantly adapted to ensure optimum performance, the security of sensitive medical data, and user satisfaction. Here are a few points that highlight the specific issues that make updates essential:

- **Security and Compliance**: Updates address emerging security vulnerabilities, ensuring the confidentiality and integrity of healthcare data, in compliance with current regulations.

- **Bug fixes**: Updates resolve bugs and technical issues that can affect application performance, ensuring an optimal user experience and avoiding potential errors in critical functionality.

- **Feature enhancement**: Technological developments and user feedback enable us to add new features, improve application efficiency and respond to changing user needs.

- **Adaptation to new technologies**: Updates allow us to adopt the latest technological advances, such as the integration of health sensors, the exploitation of artificial intelligence, or optimization for new devices.

- **Maintaining reliability**: Changes in operating systems and mobile environments can affect application stability. Updates ensure compatibility and reliability on new platforms.

- **Ongoing user engagement**: Users appreciate applications that evolve and improve. Regular updates demonstrate the developer's commitment to quality and relevance.

- **Performance Optimization**: Updates optimize application performance, reducing loading times and improving responsiveness, contributing to a better user experience.

- **Correction of Healthcare-related vulnerabilities**: In the eHealth sector, where data confidentiality is paramount, updates are essential to respond to new threats and protect sensitive medical information.

In short, regular updating of an eHealth application is essential to ensure its performance, security, and suitability for evolving user needs and regulatory requirements. This contributes to user confidence and the overall success of the application.

Chapter 5: Introducing my eCentre Convivial digital project

The eCentre Convivial Platform is a comprehensive initiative, combining various solutions to promote information and access to sexual and reproductive health services for young people and adolescents in Togo. It encompasses a mobile and web application, an automated Chatbot on WhatsApp, a Green Line, and offers a wide range of services.

Among its main features, the :

- **Adapted Sex Education Services:** The application offers adapted sex education services, including downloadable PDF and audio modules. These modules are available in several languages, including French, Ewe and Kabyè. This feature aims to provide comprehensive and accessible information on sex education, tailored to the needs of young people and adolescents.

- **Online Appointments**: This innovative feature enables young users to book appointments online for consultations related to sexually transmitted infections (STIs), family planning (FP) or voluntary HIV testing. Thanks to an ingenious geolocation system, the application automatically alerts health facility staff to the user's imminent arrival, facilitating rapid and efficient care. It also integrates the receipt of test results and medical prescriptions, simplifying medical follow-up. In addition, this functionality generates digitized cards with NFC technology, enabling beneficiaries to receive consultations in all partner health centers, reinforcing the portability of healthcare services.

- **Pregnancy, menstrual cycle and contraception tracking**: The application offers pregnancy, menstrual cycle and contraception tracking. Thanks to SMS notifications and automated calls, users are alerted to upcoming prenatal consultations, menstrual periods, ovulation or contraceptive method renewals. This feature aims to empower pregnant women and young girls, proactively informing them about their reproductive health and facilitating family planning and menstrual management.

- **Online Assistance**: A team of telephone advisors, including doctors, gynecologists, midwives, psychologists and peer educators, is available 24/7 via instant messaging and a toll-free hotline. This online helpline enables users to ask questions, receive personalized advice and dispel concerns about their sexual and reproductive health.

- **Web Series and Quizzes**: Web series dedicated to sexual and reproductive health offer an entertaining and educational approach. These series aim to raise users' awareness of key sexual health topics, while engaging them through an attractive and accessible format. The app features interactive quizzes enabling users to test and reinforce their knowledge of sexual health.

- **Online Radio**: The platform integrates an online radio that ensures the continuous dissemination of information on sexual and reproductive health. This offers a dynamic way of keeping users informed while encouraging the right to freedom of expression in the field of sexual and reproductive health.

This ambitious digital platform integrates a variety of interactive services aimed at improving understanding of and access to sexual and reproductive health care among Togo's young population.

PART 5: OUTLOOK

Chapter 1: Future prospects for a digital application

Aspiring to high ambitions is the bedrock of every innovator's journey. It's the driving force that stimulates creativity, encourages the pushing of boundaries and inspires inexhaustible energy in the pursuit of innovative ideas. However, having big ambitions requires more than just a vision; it also requires determined action to mobilize the resources needed to make those bold dreams a reality. The innovator must be a strategist, capable of identifying and maximizing the resources needed to turn his or her ambitions into reality. This often involves seeking funding, creating strategic partnerships, and mobilizing a wide range of skills. A proactive approach to mobilizing resources also includes a thorough understanding of the economic, social and technological context, as well as the ability to anticipate and overcome potential obstacles.

It's crucial for the innovator to cultivate a resilient, action-oriented mindset. Mobilizing resources is not limited to financial aspects, but also encompasses building strong teams, leveraging professional networks, and creating an environment conducive to innovation. Constant dialogue with stakeholders, both internal and external, ensures that resources are continually aligned with the innovator's ambitious goals. In short, having lofty ambitions as an innovator goes beyond mere daydreaming.

Chapter 2: Perspectives on the eCentre Convivial platform

The implementation of my innovation, which remains groundbreaking in the field, is currently at the heart of a popularization process aimed at extending the impact of this solution, with the first stage concentrated within the Economic Community of West African States (ECOWAS). This strategic approach is motivated by the desire to consolidate and maximize the positive influence of innovation in a region where the need for innovative solutions is particularly relevant. As such, the current outreach phase represents a crucial strategic step in the deployment of my innovation, aimed at extending its positive impact across the sub-region, with an initial focus on ECOWAS.

Over the last five years of experience, the application I have developed has exclusively benefited my country, Togo. I can confidently state that this solution has proven its effectiveness and has made a significant contribution to achieving the objectives set. However, this deliberate choice to initially focus the application's impact at national level was not only a strategy to meet local needs, but also a considered approach to mastering the various issues related to the field, and acquiring the skills and knowledge necessary to envisage an international reach. By concentrating the application within the Togolese context, I was able to closely observe the specific dynamics of the sector, identify local challenges and fine-tune the solution for optimal match with the real needs of the population.

At the same time, this approach served as a learning laboratory, enabling me to acquire in-depth knowledge of the particularities of the field in the Togolese context. Mastering the regulatory, cultural and technological aspects specific to my country was a necessary preliminary step before considering international expansion.

In terms of business models, it is imperative to recognize that the African context presents significant limitations, particularly when it comes to incorporating fintech components. In the face of these challenges, mobile money services are emerging as a crucial alternative, offering innovators the opportunity to offer fee-based services to users. The use of mobile money solutions represents an ingenious response to the economic constraints specific to the region. Mobile payment systems offer increased accessibility, bypassing the traditional barriers associated with bancarization and enabling a greater number of individuals to carry out financial transactions via their cell phones.

In addition, setting up a branch of my company in France was a strategic move, making my business a French entity while retaining its status as a foreign company. This initiative has opened significant doors, enabling me to establish myself on renowned financial transaction platforms such as PayPal Business, as well as leading online stores such as Amazon Sellers.

Thus, the combination of setting up a branch in France, integrating on renowned platforms, acquiring APIs for mobile payments, and taking paid services into account, converges towards a strategic international opening. These actions position the application to meet the requirements of varied markets, while offering paid services that reinforce its economic viability and global expansion.

PART 6: MOBILIZING RESOURCES

Chapter 1: The importance of resource mobilization

Resource mobilization is crucial in a digital application development project for several reasons:

- **Financing**: Securing adequate financial resources is essential to fund the costs associated with application development, including developer salaries, equipment purchases, software licenses and other associated expenses.

- **Human skills**: Mobilizing a competent team of developers, designers, testers and other professionals is essential to guarantee the success of the project. A wide range of skills is needed to cover all aspects of development.

- **Technical infrastructure**: Having the right hardware and software resources, including servers, development tools and test environments, is crucial to ensuring a smooth and efficient development process.

- **Time management**: The mobilization of time resources is necessary to establish realistic schedules and ensure effective time management. This includes planning development phases, tests and launches.

- **Risk management**: Resources are also mobilized to identify and manage potential risks. This involves putting in place mitigation plans and workarounds in the event of unexpected problems.

- **Communication and collaboration**: Mobilizing human resources facilitates communication and collaboration within the development team. Effective coordination helps avoid misunderstandings and delays.

- **Scalability**: By mobilizing scalable resources, the project can adapt to changing needs and market developments. This helps you stay competitive and meet changing user demands.

In short, the mobilization of resources - be they financial, human, technical or time-related - is essential to ensure the success of a digital application development project, by guaranteeing efficient execution, high product quality and an adequate response to the challenges encountered.

Chapter 2: Financial resources

The mobilization of financial resources is of crucial importance in the development of a digital application. These financial resources are essential to finance the entire development process, including the design, programming, testing and deployment phases of the application. In addition, they enable us to attract and maintain a talented team, by covering the competitive salaries, benefits and ongoing training of the professionals involved in the project.

Investing in the right tools and technologies is another essential facet. This includes the acquisition of development software, licenses and sometimes hardware infrastructure to guarantee the efficiency of the creation process. Mobilizing financial resources also plays a decisive role in implementing marketing and promotional strategies aimed at increasing the application's visibility and reaching a wider target audience.

Beyond initial development, these resources are needed to support ongoing activities such as testing, quality assurance, maintenance and application updates. They provide the flexibility required for risk management, enabling mitigation plans to be put in place in the face of unforeseen challenges or changes in plans. Finally, compliance with current standards and regulations may also require financial investment, in particular to implement security and data protection measures. Thus, mobilizing financial resources is a key element in ensuring the success and longevity of a digital application project in the marketplace.

Chapter 3: Strategies for mobilizing financial resources

Mobilizing financial resources for an application developer can be based on several strategies:

- **Own financing**: The developer can invest his own funds in the project. This demonstrates the developer's commitment to the project, and may also make it easier to obtain other financing.

- **Crowdfunding**: By soliciting the support of an online community, the developer can raise funds via crowdfunding platforms. This can generate initial funding and create early interest in the application.

- **Private investors**: Finding private investors interested in the project can provide substantial funding. Investors can be wealthy individuals, entrepreneurs or venture capitalists.

- **Grants and competitions**: Exploring opportunities for government, regional or sectoral grants, as well as participating in competitions, can bring non-repayable funding and increased visibility.

- **Bank loan**: If the developer has solid financial credibility, he may consider a bank loan to finance the project. However, this implies repayment of the loan with interest.

- **Strategic partnerships**: Establishing partnerships with other companies or organizations can bring funding, resources or in-kind benefits in exchange for collaboration.

- **Incubator and gas pedal programs**: Participating in incubator or gas pedal programs can offer funding, advice and resources in exchange for program participation.

- **Pre-sales and licenses**: Offering pre-sales of the application or early licenses to potential customers can generate revenue even before the official launch.

- **Venture capital**: If the project has strong growth potential, venture capitalists may be interested in providing funds in exchange for an equity stake.

- **Online lending platforms**: Using peer-to-peer or online lending platforms can be an option for obtaining funds quickly, although this involves interest rates to be repaid.

- **Monetization**: Offering paid application services can also generate significant revenue for the project.

By judiciously combining these strategies according to the nature of the project and financial requirements, an app developer can maximize his chances of mobilizing the resources needed to successfully develop and implement his app.

Chapter 4: My success in mobilizing resources

Navigating with determination in the complex world of innovative project development, I took charge of my organization's resource mobilization strategy. This involved a number of steps, including seeking grants from partners committed to promoting sexual and reproductive health. At the same time, I seized the opportunity to take part in competitions dedicated to digital innovation, seeking to obtain funding and increased visibility for my project.

Aware of the value of the data generated by my application, I also explored the possibility of monetizing this information. By considering the sale of data to relevant partners, I sought to diversify the sources of funding for my project while guaranteeing its financial sustainability. This multi-dimensional approach enabled me to strengthen the economic stability of my initiative while pursuing my goal of providing accessible and innovative sexual and reproductive health services.

The resource mobilization strategy I've undertaken rests fundamentally on one crucial pillar: the business model. This document, of paramount importance for any digital developer, details precisely how the application could generate revenue and become financially profitable. It's an essential reference, often demanded by potential partners in the search for funding.

Chapter 5: Equity financing

My resource mobilization strategies were designed with several key elements in mind. First, I invested my own funds to initiate the development of the application.

Thanks to my personal skills, I was able to offer students visual design and proofreading services for dissertation documents. I was also in demand as a consultant and trainer for various projects. These private initiatives provided me with my own funds, which I then invested in the implementation of my project. At the same time, my organization also benefited from its own funds, helping to balance the necessary finances. This approach enabled me to demonstrate my personal commitment to the project and kick-start its realization.

Chapter 6: Subsidies from United Nations system agencies

At the same time, I sought grants from various partners. UNFPA, with whom I had established a relationship of trust through previous collaborations, proved to be a key partner. Thanks to its cooperation program with the Togolese government, I was able to benefit from substantial subsidies.

The integration of my application into the Tech4Youth program, supported by UNFPA, was a decisive step in its development. Tech4Youth is a digital initiative involving five countries: Benin, Burkina Faso, Ghana, Nigeria and Togo. Spearheaded by the Innovation Office at UNFPA headquarters and led by Benin, this initiative has brought competitive recognition to the eCentre Convivial application. Thanks to Tech4Youth, the application was awarded the enviable 3-star status in terms of business model, placing it at the top of the list of competing applications. This recognition not only boosted the app's credibility, but also paved the way for a substantial grant.

The commitment and support of various United Nations entities have greatly contributed to the financial viability of the eCentre Convivial application. UNAIDS and UNDP played a key role by providing substantial grants. These combined grants represented significant financial support over the five years of the application's existence. These funds have enabled the application to broaden its impact and strengthen its role in the field of digital health.

This remarkable ability to mobilize resources has firmly positioned the eCentre Convivial application as a pioneer in the field of eHealth, not only in Togo, but also in the sub-region. Successful collaboration with partners such as UNFPA, UNAIDS and UNDP testifies to the recognition of the value and impact of this digital innovation in the field of sexual and reproductive health. This privileged position offers the application continued opportunities for growth and expansion, reinforcing its crucial role in promoting digital health.

Chapter 7: NFM2 & 3 grant (Global Fund)

As part of its 2018-2020 grant to Togo, the Global Fund recommended that our country reformulate the youth project by proposing an innovative approach. This led to consultations with the various actors involved in promoting the sexual and reproductive health of adolescents and young people in Togo, encompassing several decentralized departments of the Ministry of Health. It was in this context that the eCentre Convivial platform was approved in principle by the fund, which subsequently led to the reformulation of the youth component of the grant. This funding was a powerful catalyst for the application's growth, contributing significantly to the finalization of the development process.

During its second funding cycle, the application was renewed, this time through a service contract. This approach enabled us to sell the data generated by the application to the State, thus establishing a codified data management system.

Thanks to a grant from the Global Fund, the application has succeeded in contributing around 90% of national data on sexual and reproductive health. This significant involvement underlines the crucial importance of this digital solution in strengthening national policy efforts in this area.

Chapter 8: Competitions/Challenges

My involvement in several competitions and challenges, notably those organized by international institutions, foundations and governmental organizations, has enabled me to win significant prizes. These competitions have been crucial platforms for showcasing innovation and demonstrating its positive impact, opening up new opportunities and collaborations.

Over the course of my entrepreneurial career, I've had the opportunity to take part in various competitions that have enriched the eCentre Convivial application experience. My commitments in this area have been :

- *Lab ARA* (2018), an African competition where my eHealth initiative distinguished itself by being among the Togolese Top 3. This recognition enabled me to represent Togo at the finals in Côte d'Ivoire in 2018, positioning the app within a continental competition. Although we didn't win, this experience was a very first step in the app's development.

- *Pitch GAAT* (2018), a competition dedicated to the presentation of innovative projects and initiated by the Association of Alumni of American Government Exchange Programs. As an alumnus of these programs, I seized this opportunity funded by the U.S. Embassy to showcase my project. At the end of the Pitch GAAT competition, I was honored to win the $500 First Prize. This success marked the very first award for my eCentre Convivial application. At this stage, the monetary value of the prize was not my main concern. What was more significant for me was the recognition and distinction of my initiative among a range of other projects, confirming the quality of the work in progress.

- ***Innov4Health*** (2018), initiated by the Ministry of Health and UNDP, represented a crucial opportunity. The aim of this competition was to identify innovative solutions for monitoring pregnant women and vulnerable people in Togo. Throughout the various phases of the competition, I chose to emphasize the pregnancy monitoring and online assistance aspects of my project, concretizing them in a separate application that I named eConvivial CPN. This strategic choice was motivated by a desire to respond specifically to the needs of the competition and maximize the chances of success. Having won the €1,500 First Prize in the Innov4Health challenge, we now have significant recognition of our competitive positioning. As we progressed towards greater recognition from partners, we felt a growing responsibility to deliver concrete results and satisfaction for all stakeholders.

- **ODESS Prize** (2020): The Observatoire de la eSanté dans les pays du Sud (ODESS) is an initiative of the Pierre Fabre Foundation that aims to support high-potential digital healthcare projects in Africa and Asia. The aim of this initiative is to understand, analyze, encourage and support digital innovations for healthcare in these countries. The call is aimed at project leaders who use information and communication technologies to improve access to healthcare. Successful projects will be listed on the ODESS website. It is in this context that I have also positioned eCentre Convivial on the list of candidates. At the end of the competition, five innovations were identified in Africa and Asia, with my application coming in second place with €23,000 in funding.

- **Challenge des 1000 entrepreneurs africains** (2020): is an initiative launched by France on the occasion of the 2020 Africa-France Summit on sustainable cities to support the participation of 1,000 entrepreneurs from Africa and the Indian Ocean by financing their transport and accommodation. The Africa-France Summit was an opportunity for entrepreneurs to present their businesses or projects, seek financing and partners, and express their innovations and concerns. 1,000 African entrepreneurs, including 28 from Togo, were selected, including eCentre Convivial. During our participation in the Africa-France Summit held in

Montpellier, France, I was the only young African innovator to take part in the Choose Africa conference, alongside two major business leaders such as the Managing Director of Innovie and Bertrant, all resident in France. It was an opportunity I seized to strengthen my partnership with the Innovie laboratory, and at the same time, I had the honor of creating the branch of my startup in France, paving the way for several opportunities.

- **TOYP** (2021): TOYP (Ten Outstanding Young Persons), a program of Junior Chamber International (JCI) Togo, annually celebrates ten committed young citizens who embody the spirit of the JCI Mission. They stand out as inspirations for entrepreneurship and ethical leadership, and their personal stories of discovery, determination and ingenuity inspire members to work for a more equitable and sustainable society. That's how I came to be nominated and win the award in the Medical Innovation category. Although this competition did not come with any financial support, it nevertheless raised the profile of my innovation and ranked me among the top 10 young people of the year.

- **Scholarship in eHealth** (2021): My transition from amateur to professional took shape thanks to my participation in a call for applications initiated by the Pierre Fabre Foundation. The aim of this call was to support African innovators and decision-makers by strengthening their skills in the field of eHealth. I was selected as one of 17 African innovators to benefit from a scholarship offering intensive university courses in eHealth. Among the recipients in Togo, there were two of us, including an executive from the Ministry of Health. After several weeks of online courses, the training culminated in a reunion at the Université des Sciences, des Techniques et des Technologies de Bamako (USTTB) in Mali. This intensive program culminated in the award of an Inter-University Diploma (DIU). Our course at this university was also made possible thanks to additional financial support from the UNDP. This financial support helped to facilitate our participation in this university training program in eHealth, reinforcing our skills in the field.

- **Tadamon Accelerator** (2022): is a program based on an innovative partnership approach bringing together national and international civil society organizations, philanthropic bodies, foundations, governments and participatory financing platforms. The aim is to share knowledge, mobilize support and communicate more effectively. Civil society organizations (CSOs) participating in the Tadamon 2022 Accelerator, jointly organized by the Islamic Development Bank (IDB), the Islamic Solidarity Fund for Development (ISFD), and the United Nations Development Programme (UNDP), benefit from six weeks of intensive training and mentoring. In Togo, two organizations, including mine, were selected from among the 50 in Africa, and in the end, I was the only one to represent the country at the final project presentation phase. The results of this call for projects are still awaited as I write this book.

Beyond the mobilization of resources, ensuring the sustainability of a digital solution goes beyond its initial design. The integration of local maintenance and support mechanisms is of crucial importance. Training staff ensures ongoing technical management, while establishing accessible support channels ensures ongoing assistance to users.

Collaboration with local governments and health organizations strengthens the legitimacy and institutional anchoring of the solution. Involving communities right from the start of the design process is equally essential. This participatory approach ensures a better understanding of local needs, thus promoting long-term acceptance and use.

Financial sustainability can be supported by business models adapted to the African context. Public-private partnerships offer a viable way of combining government resources with private-sector expertise. Results-based approaches, where investments are linked to specific performance, can also ensure efficient use of resources.

In short, to ensure the sustainability of a digital solution in Africa, it's essential to adopt a holistic approach incorporating local training, institutional collaboration, participatory design and context-appropriate business models.

PART 7: ANALYSIS OF MY EXPERIENCE IN THE FIELD OF HEALTH IN AFRICA

Chapter 1: In-depth analysis of the eHealth context in Africa

Demographic growth in Africa poses significant challenges to the healthcare system, accentuated by difficulties linked to financing, training and infrastructure. Unequal access to healthcare is often exacerbated by unevenly distributed populations, creating barriers to effective care. Lack of funding limits the ability of healthcare systems to meet growing demand, while shortcomings in training can affect the quality of care. Inadequate infrastructure hampers the provision of medical services in certain regions, particularly remote areas.

Although efforts have been made by public and private institutions to develop healthcare policies, direct care of the population to the last mile remains a challenge. Innovative solutions, such as eHealth and telemedicine, can play a crucial role in overcoming these obstacles by enabling greater accessibility to healthcare services, particularly in remote areas. To meet these challenges, a comprehensive approach involving targeted investment in infrastructure, increased healthcare budgets and appropriate training programs is required. Collaboration between the public and private sectors, as well as effective coordination between the various stakeholders, is also essential to improve direct last-mile care and strengthen the healthcare system as a whole. Indeed, universal access to healthcare and information is a major concern, and technological innovations, particularly in the field of eHealth, offer innovative solutions in response. These advances enable us to connect people to new healthcare services, representing an effective way of solving the "last mile" challenge.

Digital tools, such as telemedicine applications, mobile healthcare platforms and electronic medical databases, help to reduce geographical barriers by providing remote healthcare services. This approach reintegrates populations by eliminating barriers linked to physical distance and facilitating access to essential medical information. eHealth also improves disease prevention through online information campaigns and health monitoring tools. By connecting individuals to healthcare professionals via digital platforms, these innovations help to broaden access to care and strengthen the management of medical resources. In short, innovative eHealth solutions play a crucial role in overcoming barriers to universal access to healthcare and medical information, by reintegrating populations via digital tools and thus helping to bridge the "last mile".

The challenges of infant and maternal mortality, sexually transmitted diseases, diabetes, cardiovascular disease, respiratory disorders, cancers and epidemics call for collective action. Start-ups often provide innovative solutions through mobile applications, health monitoring devices or awareness-raising platforms. With the growing number of smartphone users on the continent, these digital solutions offer a unique opportunity to reach a wide audience, particularly in areas where access to traditional healthcare is limited. By taking advantage of these different approaches, a well-coordinated collective intervention can make a significant contribution to preventing disease and improving overall health on the African continent. eHealth in Africa has significant potential to bridge the healthcare gap, particularly in remote areas where access to medical services can be limited. Initiatives such as mobile applications for telemedicine have shown promising progress in enabling remote consultation and medical data collection.

However, several challenges stand in the way of wider adoption. Limited infrastructure, including uneven access to electricity, poses technical obstacles. In addition, uneven internet connectivity in some regions hinders the effective implementation of digital solutions. To overcome these challenges, close collaboration between governments, the private sector and healthcare stakeholders is crucial. Governments can play a key role by investing in digital infrastructure, creating enabling policies and facilitating coordination between different stakeholders. The private sector can contribute by developing technologies adapted to the African context, while local healthcare players need to be involved to ensure cultural understanding and community acceptance.

It is therefore essential to take cultural and linguistic diversity into account when deploying eHealth solutions. An inclusive approach that incorporates the needs and perspectives of local communities promotes smoother adoption. In short, while eHealth in Africa holds great promise, a collaborative, adaptive and locally-focused approach is needed to overcome barriers and ensure the long-term success of these initiatives.

Chapter 2: Specificities in the development of my project

As the project grew, it became imperative to strengthen its institutional base. With this in mind, I decided to set up a company, thus adding a new dimension to the institutional anchoring of the eCentre Convivial Platform. This double dimension, both association and company, has enabled us to reconcile the social aspects of the project with a solid entrepreneurial structure, thus promoting efficient and sustainable management. The association continues to play an essential role in promoting the project's social values, while the company offers the stability needed to ensure its sustainability and expansion. This evolution in institutional structure has provided an appropriate response to the demands of the entrepreneurial environment. By creating the eConvivial company, I was able to better align the project with the standards and expectations of investors and partners in the private sector. It also opened up new opportunities in terms of financing and partnerships with private companies and organizations.

In this way, the Platform has successfully navigated between the two worlds of the socially-oriented association and the entrepreneurial company. Indeed, although subsidies played a crucial role in the project's start-up and initial development, they were no guarantee of a long-term solution. The financial viability of the project required a more entrepreneurial approach. The company now offers the possibility of providing paid services while continuing to serve its social mission. This move towards a commercial structure has created a more solid financial base, enabling the project to reduce its dependence on external funding and explore sustainable business models.

The project also stands out for its multi-channel strategy, offering users a variety of ways to access its services. Whether through the web, mobile applications, the Green Line or social networks, notably the Whatsapp automated Chatbot, the aim is to guarantee maximum accessibility to reach a variety of beneficiaries. This thoughtful approach aims to adapt to the preferences and habits of diverse users. Some may prefer the web interface, while others may find it more convenient to use the mobile application, or on the other hand those without an internet connection can go through the green line channel. A presence on social networks, particularly via Whatsapp, enables us to reach a wider audience and encourage more direct interaction.

Chapter 3: Obstacles encountered in developing my project

The initial phase of my journey as initiator and promoter of this project was marked by major challenges, the first of which related to the developers' understanding and appropriation of the concept. Overcoming this obstacle required perseverance and communication skills to effectively convey my ideas and vision of the project. The complexity of the sexual and reproductive health field required clear and precise communication to ensure a thorough understanding of the application's mission. The developers, being key players in the realization of this vision, needed to fully integrate the project objectives to ensure the successful development of the project. This first hurdle was overcome through open dialogue, clarification of expectations and close collaboration with the development team.

Mobilizing financial resources was a crucial step in my journey as initiator of this project. The very essence of the project depended on the availability of financial resources, which in turn influenced my ability to mobilize human resources. Faced with the lack of funding, I had to work day and night to find funding opportunities and develop solid business cases to present the project. The search for funding was a major challenge, requiring a thorough understanding of funding mechanisms, potential partnerships and eligibility criteria. Preparing solid presentation files was crucial to convincing potential funders of the project's value and impact. This phase required a combination of communication skills, fundraising and strategic planning. Each funding opportunity explored was a step towards making the project a reality, and this process helped develop expertise in mobilizing financial resources to support the initiative.

Security and data management have been major concerns throughout my career. Initially, I was confronted with situations where my database data would mysteriously disappear, followed by messages demanding payment of a bitcoin sum for its return. This threat, known as ransomware, required extensive research to understand and remedy its nature. To reinforce security, I implemented protective measures not only for the server, but also for the database, by introducing two-factor protocols. This approach improved resilience in the face of potential attacks and guaranteed the confidentiality and integrity of stored data. Proactive data security management is crucial in today's digital environment, where online threats can compromise the continuity and credibility of a project. Constant vigilance and adaptation to new security techniques are essential to preserve data integrity and user confidence.

The management of malicious aspects within the company is unavoidable, and I have had to deal with ill-intentioned individuals seeking to hinder the progress of my initiative. Some, due to misunderstandings or limited access to sensitive information, may have invented unfounded stories to harm the project. However, my ability to manage and balance the project rested mainly on professional secrecy and the rigorous protection of my source codes. Source code confidentiality played a crucial role in preserving the integrity of the application. By maintaining a high level of security around this sensitive information, I was able to minimize the risks associated with external attacks. The confidence of partners, users and authorities was strengthened thanks to this approach, underlining the importance of protecting digital assets in the field of innovation.

Chapter 4: Presenting the results of your work or research: an approach to visibility and networking

Celebrating successes and promoting personal initiatives also involves writing and submitting abstracts to various conferences and meetings. This not only enables us to share our achievements, but also to increase the visibility and recognition of our projects at different levels, thereby promoting the wider dissemination of innovative ideas. Submitting abstracts to conferences is of major strategic importance for innovators, researchers, practitioners and experts. By presenting your work and research results, you will benefit from international visibility, strengthening your reputation in your field. This promotes knowledge sharing, stimulates networking with peers and potential collaborators, and offers opportunities for publication in official proceedings. Throughout my career, I have devoted significant effort to writing and submitting abstracts, particularly in the field of eHealth. These articles, carefully crafted and disseminated, have played a crucial role in building a solid reputation for my innovation, contributing to its visibility and recognition in the various fields in which I operate.

Here are four articles I'd like to share from two major international conferences on sexual and reproductive health and eHealth. These conferences include the AfraVIH Conference, organized every two years on a rotating basis between a city in France and an African country, and the ICASA Conference, also held every two years in Africa. These contributions aim to enrich dialogue and promote advances in these crucial areas.

Abstract 1 : Advocacy for the creation of a digital application for sexual health and medical follow-up of PLWHA: the case of Togo

AFRAVIH 2018 - April 4 to 7, 2018 - Bordeaux (France)
Catalogue number: 1297
Kafui Koffi Akolly, Executive Director
Association des Volontaires pour la Promotion des Jeunes (AV-Jeunes), Lomé, **Togo**

Problem*: Nowadays, with the emergence of Information and Communication Technologies (ICTs), young people and teenagers are informed about formerly taboo subjects, ask questions and indulge in sexual depravity or risks; hence the high rate of early and unwanted pregnancies, new HIV and STI infections, delinquency, etc. In the field of education and learning, the Internet is a unique and valuable source of information for all adolescents. Integrating ICTs into HIV prevention strategies would be a success factor, especially for young people.*

Description*: The Association des Volontaires pour la promotion des Jeunes (AV-Jeunes) organized an advocacy mission aimed at United Nations agencies, the Togolese government, young students and other civil society organizations, to propose a new way of contributing to the promotion of sexual and reproductive health, HIV prevention and medical follow-up for PLWHA. The mobile and web application, called e-Centre Convivial, aims to give adolescents and young people access to SRH/HIV/FP information and health care services. Downloadable from Play Store and accessible via a website, it gives users access to services such as counseling and listening, online consultation for STI management, family planning, referral and medical follow-up for PLWHA.*

In all, 17 advocacy meetings were held with United Nations agencies (UNAIDS/Togo, UNAIDS West and Central Africa Region, UNFPA/Togo and UNIDO/Togo), the Togolese government (CNLS-IST), the National Division of Youth and Adolescent Health (DNSJA) and civil society organizations (RAS+, a network of PLHIV, NGO JVS and EVD). These various meetings enabled the mobilization of nearly 5,000,000 FCFA out of the 6,750,000 needed to carry out the project, and a team of six (6) young IT and communications experts was recruited to get the work underway.

Lessons learned: There's no shortage of funding, but rather of innovation. The various advocacy meetings held with partners demonstrate the need to move from one scale to another in a project's sustainability process.

Next steps: The next stage of the project is the official start of the work of the web and mobile developers, which will take place for January 16, 2018 in the presence of the partners. Once the app is online, a second stage of advocacy and resource mobilization will begin with a view to popularizing the product in the West-Central African sub-region.

Abstract 2 : The use of social networks for HIV prevention and sexual health promotion in Togo: the case of the Facebook page Santé Sexuelle et reproductive; parlons-en et sans Tabou (Sexual and reproductive health: let's talk about it without taboos)

ICACA 2019 - December 2 to 7, 2019 - Kigali (Rwanda)
Reference : A-1099-0189-02043 :
Kafui Koffi Akolly, Executive Director
Association des Volontaires pour la Promotion des Jeunes (AV-Jeunes), Lomé, Togo

Questions*: In a very short space of time, social networks have changed the way humans interact. From now on, their communication has partially moved into the virtual sphere. Social networks remain most popular with younger generations, with 90% of people aged 18 to 29 routinely using these sites (Revue québécoise de psychologie, 38, (2), 167-182). In Togo, with the emergence of information and communication technologies, leading to the existence of several social networks, notably Facebook, young people and teenagers are informed about taboo subjects and ask themselves questions.*

Methodology*: As part of the promotion of access to STI/HIV information, the AV-Jeunes association has benefited since 2017 from financial support from UNFPA for the animation of the Facebook page entitled:* **Santé Sexuelle et Reproductive; parlons-en et sans Tabou**. *A technical core to manage this page has been set up. an annual action plan defining the various articles is drawn up. Each month, the page publishes an article on sexual health, STIs or HIV, and targets, through sponsorship, the youth age group (18-24 and 25-34) in Togo's six regions. A WhatsApp link has been integrated into each article to enable web users to interact by sending messages directly to the telephone advisors to ask questions and get answers.*

Lessons learned*: As ICTs continue to emerge among young people, it's clear that we can no longer divert their attention to traditional initiatives. Hence the need to meet them on the web and give them access to the information they need. After 18 months' experience, 14,871 people have subscribed to the* *page, 88% of them Togolese Internet users; 23 sponsored articles have reached 1,615,479 young people aged 14 to 34, 68% of them male and 32% female. The total cost of the project over the 18 months is estimated at 1,560,000 FCFA.*

Next steps*: This Facebook page will be scaled up to reach at least 50,000 subscribers by the end of 2019.*

Abstract 3 : eHealth to facilitate young people's access to STI counseling, screening and management services: the case of the eCentre Convivial application in Togo

ICACA 2019 - December 2 to 7, 2019 - Kigali (Rwanda)
Catalogue number: 1099-0133-00631
Kafui Koffi Akolly, Executive Director
Association des Volontaires pour la Promotion des Jeunes (AV-Jeunes), Lomé, **Togo**

Questions: In Togo, the existence of 35 youth-friendly centers is a strategy for promoting actions concerning the health of young people and adolescents. (UNFPA Togo study, 2013). Adolescents express the desire to benefit from sex education and to have a referee with whom to talk about sexual problems, but with respect for confidentiality (Vodiena G., et al, 2012, p. 403- 415). How can the emergence of Information and Communication Technologies improve young people's health? This is what the eCentre Convivial mobile application in Togo is trying to offer.

Methodology: The Association des Volontaires pour la Promotion des Jeunes (AV-Jeunes), with support from UNFPA/Togo and the Global Fund, has developed a mobile and web-based eHealth application to improve access to STI/HIV information and care services for young people and adolescents. Two national consultants have been recruited to map 46 friendly centers and public health facilities, which are then linked to a mobile application called eCentre Convivial. Young people are then sensitized, through door-to-door awareness-raising campaigns, in schools or on social networks, for online consultation. Following the online consultation, young people are referred by their geographical location to the nearest health facility. After the consultation, they receive their prescriptions online and personalized follow-up.

Lessons learned: At the end of the 6-month pilot phase, 317 young people aged 15-24, 65% of whom were girls, used the application to visit a health center. Of these, 76 young people had instant discussions with teleconsultants; 30% were registered for lower abdominal pain; 25% for *vaginal and urethral discharge; while 20% for HIV testing; 15% for pain during intercourse and 10% for menstrual problems.*

Next steps: *Advocacy for the provision of free adapted services for young people and adolescents in health facilities.*

Abstract 4 : Technological innovation for STI/HIV prevention among young people in Togo: the case of the eCentre Convivial mobile and Web application

AFRAVIH 2020 - November 8-11, 2020 - Dakar (Senegal)
Catalogue number: 2000166
Kafui Koffi Akolly, Executive Director
Association des Volontaires pour la Promotion des Jeunes (AV-Jeunes), Lomé, **Togo**

Problem: *In Togo, the HIV prevalence rate is currently estimated at 2.1%, and among the age groups most affected are young girls aged between 13 and 24. According to the EDS III, 2014 report, only 49.6% of girls and 64% of boys aged 15-24 used condoms during their last sexual intercourse. We also note that the fertility rate among Youth and Adolescents (JA) is 84 per thousand in the 15- 19 age group compared with a global average of 47.1%. This situation represents a loss of earnings for the economy and national development in terms of healthcare costs and school dropouts. What can be done to innovate prevention and service provision in a context where young people are permanently connected to the Internet?*

Description*: As part of the Global Fund's NFM2 and NFM3 grants to Togo, the life skills of young people and adolescents were strengthened through the use of an eHealth innovation called the eCentre Convivial platform. Available in Play Store and accessible at https://www.econvivial.org, this platform has also been supported by UNFPA, UNAIDS, UNDP, CNLS-IST and the French Embassy in Togo. The NFM3 grant, covering the period 2021-2023, provides for : capacity-building for 224 peer educators on sexual and reproductive health (SRH), as well as the use of the eConvivial tool for data reporting; the use of an automated whatsapp chatbot for the dissemination of SRH/STI/HIV resources, a digital campaign around the application (sms, mail, Facebook Ads, WhatsApp, Google Ads, Twitter Ads) and the provision of online assistance services by teleconsultants thanks to instant messaging or the toll-free number 8203.*

In 2022, this application served a total of 601.466 young people and teenagers aged 10-24, 82.8% of them girls, on topics such as: Online assistance (19.85%), Sexual abstinence (1.53%), STI/HIV (34.86%), Female condom (0.23%), Menstrual cycle (0.02%), Male condom (19.86%), Early and unwanted pregnancy (15.13%), Contraceptive method (2.83%), Sexual and menstrual hygiene (5.29%) and COVID-19 (0.40%). The eConvivial platform was awarded the Prix de la eSanté ODESS 2020 by the Pierre Fabre Foundation, the Prix de l'Innovation médicale 2021 by the Jeune Chambre International Togo and the Prix Innov4Health by the UNDP.

Lessons learned: *reducing new HIV infections starts with understanding young people's needs and offering services tailored to them, while bringing the service closer to them.*

Next steps: *Deployment of the eCentre Convivial platform in ECOWAS countries and implementation of the business model.*

Chapter 5: Learning from success

The success of a digital project hinges on a thorough command of the subject matter, an in-depth understanding of the theme in question, and advanced knowledge of technical aspects and computer codes. This combination of skills enables the project manager to make informed decisions, effectively direct the development of the application, and ensure coherence between the project vision and its concrete implementation. In-depth knowledge of the application field also enables us to better anticipate the needs of end-users, and to design digital solutions that are better adapted and more effective. The digital field is undergoing significant expansion, particularly in Africa, where new opportunities are emerging in a largely unexplored context. The emergence of innovative digital solutions is helping to transform various sectors such as healthcare, education, commerce, transport and many others, offering new prospects for the continent's economic and social development.

In Africa, the digital revolution is delivering benefits such as increased access to information, facilitating business transactions, strengthening healthcare systems, and supporting entrepreneurial initiatives. Governments, businesses and entrepreneurs are realizing the immense potential of digital technology to solve local challenges and stimulate economic growth.

The protection of personal data is a major issue in today's digital environment. Ensuring the confidentiality and security of users' personal information is a crucial responsibility for any company or organization operating in the digital sector. Implementing robust security measures, such as encrypting data, using secure transmission protocols, and rigorously managing access to sensitive information, is essential to prevent breaches of user privacy. In addition, compliance with data protection regulations, such as the General Data Protection Regulation (GDPR) in Europe, or other national laws, is essential to avoid legal sanctions and maintain user trust.

Transparency in data collection, use and storage, and the ability of users to control their own personal information, also contribute to the trust and credibility of digital platforms. The security of a digital system is an essential component in the success and sustainability of a digital project. In an ever-changing technological landscape, where cyberthreats are becoming increasingly sophisticated, guaranteeing the security of data and systems is becoming an absolute priority.

In addition, awareness-raising and training of all those involved in the project are essential. Team members need to be aware of potential risks, and trained in good IT security and confidentiality practices. This culture of security and confidentiality helps to reduce human error, which can often be a weak point. By adhering to these fundamental security principles, a digital project can better protect itself against potential threats, ensuring user confidence and the long-term success of the initiative.

Chapter 6: My role in the continued growth of this sector

As a young innovator, my role in the sector's continued growth rests on several pillars. Firstly, it's essential to cultivate an insatiable curiosity, keep abreast of the latest technological trends and explore new opportunities. Collaborating with other innovators and industry players fosters a dynamic exchange of knowledge and stimulates collective creativity. Active participation in innovation networks, conferences and mentoring initiatives offers opportunities for continuous learning.

In addition, a commitment to education and awareness-raising is crucial. Sharing my experience, promoting the culture of innovation among younger generations and contributing to educational programs strengthens the sector's growth potential. Finally, social and ethical responsibility must guide my actions, ensuring that my innovations are rooted in sustainable values that respect society. By embracing these roles, I am helping to nurture a thriving digital ecosystem, conducive to continuous innovation and collective prosperity.

CONCLUSION

Chapter 1: Taking stock

Through the pages of this account, the review of my journey in digital innovation resonates like a symphony of learning, challenges overcome and gratifying successes. From the conception to the realization of a pioneering digital health application, each step has shaped my understanding of the digital ecosystem. Fruitful collaborations, resource mobilization strategies and constant adjustments were the cornerstones of this journey. The dual institutional roots, from association to start-up, reflect the adaptability essential to project growth. The challenges of security and data protection have taught us the crucial importance of vigilance in an ever-changing digital world. All in all, this report is a testimony to an entrepreneurial adventure in which innovation, perseverance and collaboration were the keys to success.

Chapter 2: Reflections

In light of my journey, here are a few messages for reflection that I can share:

- **The Importance of Perseverance**: My experience highlights the need for perseverance in the face of obstacles. Initial challenges with developers and mobilizing financial resources were overcome thanks to my perseverance and commitment to my vision.

- **Collaboration between Innovators and Developers**: The story of my collaboration with the developer underlines the importance of open communication and mutual understanding between innovators and developers. This close collaboration resulted in a successful application.

- **The need for a solid knowledge base**: My experience shows that success in the field of digital development hinges on in-depth knowledge of the subject. I've stressed the importance of mastering the subject of sexual and reproductive health to succeed in developing an application of this kind.

- **Digital Project Security**: My ordeal with data security highlights the crucial importance of investing in digital project security. This includes protection against cyber threats, data security and team member awareness.

- **Adaptability and evolution of the business model**: My transition from association to company shows how important it is to be adaptable in the digital field. This evolution enabled me to better meet the financial needs of the project.

- **Seeking alternative financing**: My resource mobilization strategy, including participation in competitions, emphasizes the importance of seeking alternative financing and diversifying revenue sources to ensure a project's sustainability.

- **Inclusion and Diversity of Access**: The diversity of access channels to my application, from the web to social networks to the green line, underlines the importance of making a project accessible to a wide range of beneficiaries, thus promoting greater inclusivity.

- **Valuing awards and recognition**: My participation and successes in competitions have highlighted the importance of valuing awards and recognition to reinforce a project's credibility and visibility.

- **Source code protection**: My last point highlights the need to protect source codes as a key element in the management of a digital project, thus ensuring the confidentiality and longevity of the project.

By sharing these thoughts, I inspire other digital entrepreneurs and innovators, offering valuable lessons for their own journeys.

Chapter 3: Final messages and encouragement

Here are a few final messages and words of encouragement for you, my dear readers:

- **Pursue your Vision**: Whatever field you're in, don't give up on your vision. The challenges may seem insurmountable, but perseverance and belief in your vision can take you far.

- **Believe in Collaboration**: Collaboration between innovators and developers is a key to success. Seek strong partnerships, foster open communication, and together you can realize exceptional projects.

- **Invest in your Knowledge**: Mastery of the subject is fundamental. Invest time in acquiring in-depth knowledge in your field of activity. This will boost your credibility and your ability to innovate.

- **Prioritize security**: In the digital age, data security is essential. Put robust measures in place to protect your project, your users and your data.

- **Be adaptable**: Change can be inevitable. Be ready to adapt, evolve and find creative solutions to challenges.

- **Diversify your Funding Sources**: Explore different avenues for mobilizing resources. Grants, competitions and other initiatives can help make your project financially viable.

- **Promote Inclusivity**: Make sure your project is accessible to as many people as possible. Inclusivity is not only ethical, it can also broaden the impact of your innovation.

- **Celebrate your successes**: Take the time to celebrate your successes, even the small ones. Rewards and recognition boost motivation and give visibility to your project.

- **Protect your assets**: The confidentiality of your source code is crucial. Protect your digital assets and make sure you have the appropriate mechanisms in place to guarantee the security and longevity of your project.

- **Inspire and be inspired**: Share your story to inspire other innovators, and don't hesitate to draw inspiration from the experiences of others. Entrepreneurship is a collective journey.

My journey shows that, even in the face of considerable challenges, a passionate vision, perseverance and a strategic approach can lead to the realization of exceptional projects. Best wishes to all those who aspire to create, innovate and make a positive difference in the world.

Chapter 4: Epilogue

At the dawn of this exciting adventure in the world of digital innovation, my conclusion reveals a trajectory rich in challenges, discoveries and achievements. My journey, marked by effort and determination, has culminated in the realization of an innovative application in the field of sexual and reproductive health. The lessons learned from this experience underline the importance of collaboration, continuous learning and adaptability in an ever-changing digital environment. Beyond the successes achieved, the epilogue highlights the need to maintain rigorous ethics, protect sensitive data and actively contribute to the growth of the sector. As a young innovator, my role in the continued growth of this field is clear: cultivate curiosity, share knowledge, foster inclusion and work for innovations rooted in sustainable values.

That's how one chapter ends, paving the way for new opportunities, collaborations and breakthroughs in the vast world of digital innovation. The narrative freezes, but the innovative spirit remains vibrant, ready to imagine the digital future yet to be built.

Chapter 5: Final thoughts on personal and professional development

Through this journey into the complex world of digital innovation, my final reflections revolve around the personal and professional evolution that resulted from this captivating experience. The essence of this adventure lies not only in the design of a revolutionary application, but also in the personal growth that accompanied each step.

Professionally, the course has been a catalyst for multidisciplinary skills. From working with developers to rigorous resource management, via the various training courses I had to attend, each challenge was an opportunity to learn and adjust my understanding of the ever-changing digital world. The key lay in my ability to navigate through the technical complexities while remaining aligned with the project's initial vision.

On a personal level, this journey instilled in me crucial values such as perseverance, adaptability and patience. Solving problems in real time, making crucial decisions and managing relationships with various stakeholders helped hone my leadership skills. Every obstacle was a learning ground, every success an affirmation of determination.

Ultimately, this digital odyssey has transcended the boundaries of the professional to become a personal quest for growth and fulfillment. It underscores the power of innovation to transform not only ideas into reality, but also individuals into confident pioneers ready to boldly shape the future. As such, these final reflections celebrate not only the application created, but also the person who has become in the course of this digital epic.

POSTFACE

As I begin this afterword, I would like to express my deep gratitude to all those who have perused these pages. Writing this work was much more than a simple retrospective of my journey in digital innovation; it was an invitation to share an adventure, to grasp the challenges, the successes, and the countless lessons learned.

Dear reader, perhaps you've felt the echo of reflections, the vibrancy of challenges met, or perhaps even found mirrors of your own experiences. Over the course of these chapters, I've taken you behind the scenes of the creation of an innovative application, but also into the heart of my own personal and professional growth.

This book goes beyond the simple narration of a digital project. It seeks to inspire, teach and connect with those who share my passion for innovation. The notions of perseverance, collaboration and digital security are the beacons that have guided my journey, and which I hope to share as sources of inspiration.

My wish is that these pages are not the end, but rather the beginning of new reflections, discussions and collaborations. Technologies evolve, challenges change, but the passion to create, innovate and make a difference remains.

So let this afterword be an invitation to look to the future, to embrace the unknown with courage, and to continue exploring the infinite horizons of digital innovation.

With gratitude,

Kafui Kafui AKOLLY
Writer

BIBLIOGRAPHY

[1] CNLS-IST-TOGO, "Rapport annuel des activités de lutte contre le VIH et le SIDA", 2022

[2] DIGI SANTE, "DIU eSanté, Promotion 2021, Innovation et Pratiques en Santé", 2021

[3] A. P. Koumamba, "Modèle de système d'information pour le pilotage, les statistiques et la veille sanitaire au Gabon", 2021

[4] UNAIDS, N. K. Tadegnon, "e-Health applications analysis report, 2021.

[5] UNFPA Benin, K. Hamouchi, "Business Models Analysis Tech4Youth Platforms", 2020

[6] STARTUPBRICS, J. Lanckriet, S. Abdelkrim, "Compte rendu d'enquête terrain pour l'Observatoire de la e-santé dans les pays du Sud, 2020", (https://www.odess.io/enquete/ecentre-convivial/)

[7] ODESS, "Laureate 2020 de l'Observatoire de la eSanté dans les Pays du Sud", 2020, (https://www.odess.io/initiative/ecentre-convivial/)

[8] AV-JEUNES, "Manuel de référence de la plateforme eCentre Convivial", 2020

[9] UNFPA Togo, "eConvivial: an application sponsored by UNFPA Togo in the fight against COVID-19 in Togo", 2020, (https://togo.unfpa.org/fr/news/econvivial-une-application-sponsorisee-par-unfpa-togo-dans-la-lutte-contre-le-covid-19-au-togo)

[10] RFI, "Priorité Santé, Outils numériques dans le suivi des épidémies", 2020, (https://www.rfi.fr/fr/podcasts/20201016-outils-num%C3%A9riques-le-suivi-%C3%A9pid%C3%A9mies)

[11] PARTENARIAT OUAGA, "Convivial e-Center reference manual development process launched," 2019, (https://partenariatouaga.org/le-processus-delaboration-du-manuel-de-reference-de-le-centre-convivial-lance/)

[12] ICASA 2019, "Abstract-Book-online-version", 2019, (https://saafrica.org/new/wp-content/uploads/2020/02/ICASA-2019-Abstract-Book-online-version.pdf)

[13] SAAFRICA, "Poster Track-D, ICASA 2019", 2019, (https://saafrica.org/new/wp-content/uploads/2020/04/ICASA2019_Posters_Track-D.pdf)

From Health to Code: The Epic of an Innovator in eHealth

Through the captivating pages of this book, immerse yourself in the dynamic world of digital innovation in Africa. Follow the inspiring journey of Kafui K. AKOLLY, a passionate young innovator, from the genesis of a bold idea to the realization of a revolutionary application in the field of sexual and reproductive health. The author shares in-depth reflections on the personal and professional evolution resulting from this unique experience.

Powerful messages about perseverance, collaboration, and the need for digital security resonate through every page, offering valuable lessons for budding entrepreneurs and innovators.

In conclusion, this book is not only a chronicle of digital successes, but also a personal exploration of growth, adaptability, and the transformative power of innovation. Celebrate every victory, learn from every challenge, and be inspired to boldly shape your own digital future.

KAFUI KOFFI AKOLLY born March 11, 1983, is an eHealth expert, dynamic entrepreneur and versatile musical artist. As an entrepreneur, he has made his mark in the eHealth field, bringing significant innovations. At the same time, he expresses his creativity through his music and writing.

I want morebooks!

Buy your books fast and straightforward online - at one of world's fastest growing online book stores! Environmentally sound due to Print-on-Demand technologies.

Buy your books online at
www.morebooks.shop

Kaufen Sie Ihre Bücher schnell und unkompliziert online – auf einer der am schnellsten wachsenden Buchhandelsplattformen weltweit! Dank Print-On-Demand umwelt- und ressourcenschonend produzi ert.

Bücher schneller online kaufen
www.morebooks.shop

info@omniscriptum.com
www.omniscriptum.com

Printed by Books on Demand GmbH, Norderstedt / Germany